DONGYANGBOOKS LPE Series **6**

ELEMENTARY INTENSIVE WORKBOOK **6**

Let's Play English

GRADE **6**

Lesson 09 ~ 16

SYLLABUS

Grade 6

LESSON	VOCABULARY	LOOK AND LISTEN
1 Where are you from?	Japan, America, England, Canada, Korea, Singapore, China, Australia, library, classroom, cafeteria, science lab, computer lab, music room, floor, 1st, 2nd, 3rd	A: Where are you from? B: I'm from Singapore. A: Nice to meet you.
2 Is this York Street?	bookstore, building, corner, restaurant, street, toy shop, right, left, straight, hospital, bus stop, police station, fire station, church, bank, museum, office, post, ask, behind, between, turn	A: Where is York Street? B: Go straight and turn left at the corner. A: Thank you, ma'am.
3 I like spring.	spring, warm, beautiful, summer, hot, swimming, fall, leaf, letter, winter, cold, snowman, ski, vacation, feel, leave, wait, weather	A: Do you like fall? B: Yes, I do. I like fall. How about you? A: I like spring.
4 When is your birthday?	January, February, March, April, May, June, July, August, September, October, November, December, date, New Year's Day, birthday, concert, Thanksgiving Day, Halloween Day, Christmas, last, vacation, when, why, what, who, how, where, celebrate	A: When is your birthday? B: It's May 20th. I got a bike last year.
5 May I help you?	car, helicopter, melon, watermelon, doll, soccer ball, pencil case, box, magazine, take, will, for, buy, please, some, cheap, expensive, change	A: May I help you? B: Yes. How much is that toy helicopter? A: It's $20.
6 Can I have some water?	sandwich, thirsty, water, hamburger, juice, chicken, pizza, egg, coke, bread, cookie, pie, full, sweet, taste, salty, sour, bitter, delicious, drink, try	A: Can I have some water? B: Here you are. A: Thank you. How kind of you.
7 My father is a pilot.	doctor, driver, nurse, police officer, fire fighter, teacher, cook, computer programmer, mailman, dentist, scientist, engineer, violinist, officer, pilot, singer, soldier, professor, sailor, painter, lawyer, writer, pianist, work	A: Is he your father? B: Yes, he is. He's a pilot.
8 What will you do this summer?	take a trip, go camping, go hiking, play soccer, play baseball, play basketball, play tennis, play the piano, play the violin, play the cello, play the guitar, visit, grandparents, cousin, aunt, uncle, learn	A: What will you do this summer? B: I will visit my uncle in London. A: Really? That's great.
9 How was your vacation?	vacation, camping, trip, museum, hiking, holiday, great, wonderful, fun, family, grandparents, cousin, study, watch, have a good time, visit / **5**	A: How was your vacation? B: It was wonderful! I had a good time in London. / **6**
10 I'm stronger than you.	taller, shorter, hotter, longer, faster, slower, stronger, older, younger, fatter, thinner, prettier, uglier, funnier, better, worse, more interesting, more exciting / **19**	A: I'm taller than my father. B: I'm stronger than you. A: I don't think so. / **20**
11 What do you want to do?	guitar, musical, show, talk, invite, cook, want, sing, dance, make, birthday, party, card, idea, play the piano, tomorrow / **33**	A: What do you want to do? B: I want to play the piano. / **34**
12 Will you help me, please?	airplane, bucket, paper, painting, move, paint, pass, help, will, hold, problem, tired, heavy, together / **47**	A: Will you help me with my homework? B: No problem. / **48**
13 That's too bad.	fever, earache, headache, toothache, stomachache, sick, worry, hope, soon, rest, cold, flower, dentist, nurse, magazine, get well / **61**	A: He had a bad cold. B: That's too bad. A: He will be OK soon. / **62**
14 Would you like to come to my house?	Thanksgiving day, turkey, pie, delicious, invite, eat, join, write, take off, put on, wear, try, model, fox, snake, from, prince / **75**	A: Would you like to come to my house? B: Sure, I'd love to. / **76**
15 It's time to go home.	have breakfast, have lunch, have dinner, do the dishes, go back home, go shopping, take a bus, take a bath, turn off, turn on, brush teeth, No littering, No smoking, No talking / **89**	A: It's time to go home. B: I want to skate more. / **90**
16 So long, everyone!	congratulations, farewell, middle school, high school, college, university, elementary school, kindergarten, miss, graduation, celebrate, take care of / **103**	A: We are going to the same middle school. B: That's great. So long, everyone! / **104**

EASY GRAMMAR	SING ALONG	ROLE PLAY	LET'S READ	LET'S HAVE FUN
Nation & Nationality	The more we get together	Beauty contest	Pigs	Word puzzle Snowball game
This vs. That	Do you know the muffin man?	Where is the post office?	Paris	Word puzzle Direction game
Exclamation with How / What	Did you ever see a lassie?	The ant and the grasshopper / Hansel and Gretel	Pandora's Box	Word puzzle Pop-up Words
When-Questions	Bingo	Inviting friends	The old vegetables	Word puzzle Pass or return game
How much-Questions	Hokey Pokey	At a book store / At a clothing store	Give me the money!	Word puzzle What's missing?
Can / May	This is the way.	Dinner time / At a fastfood restaurant	The best doctor	Word puzzle Something in mind
Possessive Pronouns	The farmer in the dell	What do you want to be? / What does your father do?	Whose money is it?	Word puzzle Hot envelope
Will / Be going to	A sailor went to sea.	What will you do? / What are you going to do?	Dish soap for dinner.	Word puzzle Speed sentence
Past tense / 9	Mary Had a Little Lamb / 10	Peter Pan / 11	Handsome Again? / 12	Word puzzle Snatch Sentence / 14
Comparative / 23	London Bridge / 24	The Wind And The Sun / 25	A New Man / 26	Word puzzle Pantomime / 28
To + Verb / 37	Old Macdonald / 38	What do you want to do? / 39	The Birthday Present / 40	Word puzzle Chinese Whisper / 42
Modal-Will / 51	The Merry-Go-Round / 52	Will you help me? / 53	The Coin / 54	Word puzzle Problem Solving / 56
Dialogue on the phone / 65	Skidama Rinka Dinka Dink / 66	Why don't you go see a doctor? / Take some medicine. / 67	Man's Best Friend / 68	Word puzzle Simon says / 70
Would you like to / 79	If You're Happy / 80	Little Prince / 81	Lost and Found / 82	Word puzzle Word Chain / 84
It's time to / 93	Hickory Dickory Dock / 94	It's time to study. / It's time to go to bed. / 95	Thanks a Million / 96	Word puzzle Bingo Game / 98
Be going to / 107	We Wish You a Merry Christmas / 108	Hansel and Gretel / 109	Don't Eat the Furniture / 110	Word puzzle Board Game / 112

MAIN CHARACTERS

Nami

Jenny

Jinho

Mike

Ann

Joon

Tan

Kevin

Peter

Namsu

Mrs. Smith

Mrs. Brown

HOW WAS YOUR VACATION?

1 family _____

2 grandparents _____

3 cousin _____사촌_____

4 camping _____

5 hiking _____

6 trip _____여행_____

7 museum _____

8 watch TV _____

9 study _____

♣ vacation _____

♣ holiday _____

♣ great _____훌륭한_____

♣ wonderful _____

♣ fun _____

♣ have a good time _____좋은 시간 보내다_____

♣ visit _____

Look and Listen

👀 **Listen and fill in the blanks.**

Jinho : Hi, Tan. _____ to _____ you again.

Tan : Hi, Jinho. How was your _____ ?

Jinho : It was great.

I _____ my grandparents in Busan.

Tan : Did you go _____, too?

Jinho : Yes, it was _____. How was your vacation?

Tan : It was wonderful!

I _____ a _____ time _____ London.

Jinho : How was yours, Joon?

Joon : It was not fun.

Jinho : Did you _____ English?

Joon : A _____.

Tan : Did you _____ books?

Joon : No.

Tan : Then, what did you do? Did you _____ TV?

Joon : Yes !

Look at the dialogues and speak in English.

A

 앤, 여행은 어땠니?

 으음... 재미없었어.

 왜?

 내가 아팠거든.

 정말 안됐구나.
지금은 괜찮니?

 응, 괜찮아. 고마워.

B

 안녕, 케빈. 방학은 잘 보냈니?

 재미있었어. L.A.에 사는 친척네 갔었어.

 거기서 뭐 했니?

 디즈니랜드에 갔었어.
너는 방학을 어떻게 보냈니?

 좋았어.
나는 가족과 박물관에 갔었어.

 좋았겠다.

 Let's Write

A **Listen to the dialogue again and answer the questions.**

1. Where did Jinho go during summer vacation?

2. Did Jinho go camping?

3. Where did Tan go during summer vacation?

4. Did Joon read books during vacation?

5. What did Joon do during vacation?

B **Answer these questions about yourself.**

1. What did you do during summer vacation?

2. What was the best thing?

3. What was the worst thing?

4. What do you want to do next vacation?

C **Ask these questions to your partner.**

1. Where did you go in summer?

2. What did you do?

3. Did you have a good time?

4. What do you want to do next vacation?

 **Easy Grammar**

Change the tense into the past tense.

A : I go to school.

B : I went to school.

- go / went
- study / studied
- come / came
- need / needed
- visit / visited
- like / liked
- meet / met
- read / read

1. *A* : I go camping.

   B : _____

2. *A* : I study English.

   B : _____

3. *A* : He comes from Japan.

   B : _____

4. *A* : I need a car.

   B : _____

5. *A* : She visits her family.

   B : _____

6. *A* : You like eating apples.

   B : _____

7. *A* : She meets many friends.

   B : _____

8. *A* : He reads books during vacation.

   B : _____

PETER PAN

Wendy	I'll go to school again.
Peter Pan	Hi, Wendy.
Wendy	Hi, Peter Pan.
Peter Pan	How was your holiday?
Wendy	It was not fun. I was sick.
Peter Pan	That's too bad. Are you OK now?
Wendy	Yes, I'm OK. How was your holiday?
Peter Pan	It was great. I went skating. Look, Wendy. This is for you.
Wendy	Wow!
Peter Pan	Wendy, let's fly to Neverland. We can skate there.
Wendy	Sounds good. Let's go.

Handsome Again?

Word Bank

custom 관습, 관행

pull out 뽑다

front 앞, 정면

teeth 이, 치아(tooth
의 복수형)

children 아이들

Sudan 수단

village 마을

men 남자들, 어른들

handsome 잘생긴

beautiful 아름다운

the United States
미국

problem 문제

another 또 다른 하나

soft 부드러운

hard 딱딱한

dentist 치과 의사

expensive 값비싼

There is a custom to pull the six front teeth out when children are 10 years old in Sudan. When Pantilla was ten years old, men in his village pulled six of his teeth out. People in his village said, "Men with no front teeth look handsome. Women with no front teeth look beautiful."

When Pantilla's family moved to the United States, he had a problem. Men with no six front teeth are not handsome. Women with no six front teeth are not beautiful. There was another problem. In Pantilla's village in Sudan, all the food was soft. It was easy to eat with no front teeth. But, in the United States, not all the food was soft. It was not easy to eat hard food like apples and steaks with no front teeth.

Pantilla went to the dentist to put new teeth in his mouth. It was expensive. He wanted to eat all the food. He wanted to be handsome again.

A Choose the correct answer.

1. Pantilla didn't have six of his _____ teeth.
   a. front   b. back
   c. white   d. broken

2. Pantilla lived in _____.
   a. Switzerland   b. Brazil
   c. Sudan   d. Korea

3. It's custom to pull out six front teeth when children are _____ years old.
   a. 10   b. 11
   c. 12   d. 13

4. The girls want to look beautiful, and the boys want to look _____.
   a. cute   b. handsome
   c. young   d. funny

5. It was easy to eat food in Pantilla's village because the food was _____.
   a. bad   b. hard
   c. soft   d. hot

B Find the wrong words and cross them out. Then write the correct words.

There is a ~~game~~ to pull the teeth out when children are 10 years old. → custom

1. When Pantilla's family moved to Africa, he had a problem. → _____

2. It was not easy to eat soft food with no front teeth. → _____

3. Pantilla went to the fire fighter to put new teeth in his mouth. → _____

LET'S HAVE FUN

Word Puzzle

* bad
* camping
* cousin
* dinosaur
* fly
* friend
* fun
* good
* holiday
* museum
* park
* raining
* see
* sick
* skating
* sounds
* trip
* vacation
* watch
* wonderful
* zoo
* great

W	I	G	K	O	X	Z	T	V	O	F	C	I	H	W
O	L	M	M	G	T	O	R	P	R	D	L	T	N	A
Q	G	S	U	N	E	O	W	I	I	U	T	I	K	T
N	K	J	E	I	N	K	E	N	F	R	S	T	R	C
S	F	U	S	P	T	N	G	R	X	U	T	T	A	H
P	L	O	U	M	D	D	E	F	O	B	D	G	P	S
N	Y	M	M	A	K	D	A	C	T	X	N	Z	K	S
K	D	A	B	C	N	D	V	D	G	I	V	A	C	Y
S	S	E	E	O	T	T	I	A	N	R	T	L	A	Q
U	S	O	W	B	F	N	T	I	C	I	E	D	P	Q
Y	G	O	I	T	O	F	A	E	N	A	I	A	F	K
Z	O	D	U	S	I	R	U	G	K	L	T	X	T	V
W	O	O	A	N	Q	J	Q	N	O	C	Y	I	M	Z
R	D	U	W	O	D	J	W	H	Z	B	I	H	O	P
T	R	W	Y	J	M	S	W	H	I	J	J	S	Z	N

Snatch Sentence

ACTIVITY

studying the past tense of verbs

things you need : flash cards(as many as the students)

WORD

was / did / visited / studied / played / cooked / read / watched
went camping / went swimming / went hiking / went skating

EXPRESSION

- I visited my uncle.
- I studied English.
- I went camping.

I visited my uncle.

A Use the past tense verbs and complete the sentences.

1. I _____ TV after dinner with my sister.

2. She _____ her homework in the afternoon.

3. He _____ much water after running a race.

4. We _____ hard for a test.

5. They _____ a movie *"Batman begins."*

6. You _____ your cousin in New York, right?

7. My mother _____ a new cell phone yesterday.

8. She _____ long because she was very tired.

9. I _____ rice and soup for lunch.

10. I had a big dinner because I _____ very hungry.

B Change the given verbs into the past tense.

1. I (visit) my grandparents in Busan.

2. It (is) wonderful!

3. I (go) to Disneyland last winter.

4. He (play) computer games yesterday.

5. She (watch) TV last night.

6. He (read) the book yesterday.

Write in correct order.

1. did / you / do / What /?

   _____

2. you / Did / ? / study / English

   _____

3. visited / my / cousin / L.A. / I / in

   _____

4. went / to / I / the / . / museum

   _____

5. friends / . / my / played / I / baseball / with

   _____

Listen and fill in the blanks.

Nami : Hi, Kevin. (1)_____ was your (2)_____?

Kevin : It was (3)_____.

   I (4)_____ my (5)_____ in L.A.

Nami : What (6)_____ you do there?

Kevin : I (7)_____ to Disneyland.

   How was your vacation?

Nami : It was (8)_____. I went to the (9)_____

   with my (10)_____.

Kevin : Sounds good.

PROJECT

Make sentences using the past tense.

I went to the museum last weekend.

I'm Stronger than You

1. tall-taller   키 큰-더 키 큰

2. short-shorter _____

3. hot-hotter _____

4. strong-stronger
     강한-더 강한

5. fat-fatter _____

6. slow-slower _____

7. fast-faster _____

8. pretty-prettier _____

9. heavy-heavier
     무거운-더 무거운

10. thin-thinner _____

11. ugly-uglier _____

12. long-longer _____

♣ old-older   늙은-더 늙은

♣ young-younger
     젊은-더 젊은

♣ funny-funnier _____

♣ good-better   좋은-더 좋은

♣ bad-worse _____

♣ interesting-
more interesting
     재미있는-더 재미있는

♣ exciting-more exciting

Look and Listen

👀 Listen and fill in the blanks.

Kevin : Wow! You're very _____.

Mike : Umm. I'm _____ than my father.

Kevin : Can you run _____?

Mike : Sure. I'm _____ than you.

Kevin : Are you _____?

Mike : Sure.

Kevin : What a _____!

Jenny : Mike is very _____.

Mike : Of course. I'm _____ than you.

Kevin : I don't _____ _____.

Jenny : You are _____ _____ Mike!

Mike : Yes. You're really _____.

Look and Speak

 Look at the dialogues and speak in English.

A

내 연필 어디 있지?

이게 너의 연필이니?

아니, 내 것은 그것보다 길어.

이게 너의 연필이니?

아니, 나의 연필은 그것보다 길어.

봐! 이것이 너의 연필이네.

B

너의 생일은 언제니?

12월 25일.

오우, 크리스마스가 너의 생일이네.

나미야, 너는 생일이 언제니?

9월 10일이야.
내가 너보다 더 나이가 많아.

Let's Write

A **Listen to the dialogue again and answer the questions.**

1. Is Mike taller than his father?

   _____

2. Who is stronger between Kevin and Mike?

   _____

3. Are they playing arm wrestling?

   _____

4. Who is a winner?

   _____

5. Who is a loser?

   _____

B **Answer these questions about you and your partner.**

1. Who is stronger?   _____

2. Who is taller?   _____

3. Who is shorter?   _____

4. Who is faster?   _____

5. Who is fatter?   _____

C **Write in English.**

1. Jane은 나보다 키가 크다. → _____

2. Sam은 형보다 작다.   → _____

3. 버스는 택시보다 길다. → _____

4. 엄마가 Jane보다 예쁘다. → _____

5. 아빠는 나보다 힘이 세다. → _____

 **Easy Grammar**

Change the adjective into comparative form.

I am tall.
my father   I am taller than my father.

- tall / taller
- young / younger
- big / bigger
- fast / faster
- funny / funnier
- strong / stronger
- pretty / prettier
- interesting / more interesting

1. He is young.
   his mother
   _____

2. It is big.
   the house
   _____

3. The train is fast.
   the bus
   _____

4. You are funny.
   him
   _____

5. He is strong.
   her
   _____

6. They are pretty.
   you
   _____

7. This movie is interesting.
   that movie
   _____

London Bridge

1. Lon - don Bridge is fall - ing down,

2. Build - it up with ir - on bars,

3. Ir - on bars will bend and break,

fall - ing down, fall - ing down. Lon - don Bridge is fall - ing down, my fair la - dy.

ir - on bars, ir - on bars. Build it up with ir - on bars, my fair la - dy.

bend and break, bend and break. Ir - on bars will bend and break, my fair la - dy.

THE WIND AND THE SUN

The Wind and the Sun were arguing which was the stronger.
Suddenly they saw a traveler coming down the road.

Sun   You know what? I'm bigger, prettier,
      and stronger than you.

Wind What? No, way!!
      Well, maybe you can be prettier,
      but I'm much stronger.

Sun   I have a good idea! Let's make a bet.
      Whichever takes off the traveler's
      cloak first shall be the winner. You start.

Wind Okay. I'm sure that I'm stronger than you!

The Sun hid behind a cloud, and the Wind began to blow harder and harder.
But the harder he blew, the more closely the traveler wrapped his cloak round him.
At last, the Wind had to give up in despair.

Wind It's not easy. I think I'd better give up.

Sun   It's my turn.

Then the Sun came out and shone in all his glory upon the traveler,
who soon found it too hot to walk with his cloak on.

Sun   I'm the winner! I'm stronger than you!

A New Man

Roy lives in England. Roy was very big. He weighed 500 pounds. For lunch Roy ate nine pieces of bacon, five eggs, nine potatoes, and fried vegetables. For dinner he ate beef and more vegetables, and after dinner he always ate sweets. Before he went to bed, he ate some bread and pie. Roy couldn't drive a regular car because he was too big. He couldn't sit in the front seat. Roy had a special car. Roy drove his car from the back seat.

One day the doctor said, "Roy, you need to buy a special coffin — a coffin for a very big man. You have to go on a diet, or you're going to die soon." Roy went on a diet. For breakfast he ate cereal with milk. For lunch he ate baked peas on toast. For dinner he ate fish and vegetables. After Roy began to lose weight, he met a beautiful lady. Her name was Josephine. Roy didn't stop his diet. In 24 months he lost 300 pounds. Three years later, he and Josephine got married.

Ⓐ **Choose the correct answer.**

1. What was Roy's problem?
   a. He was too big.   b. He was too handsome.
   c. He was too small.   d. He was too nice.

2. What did the doctor ask Roy to do?
   a. go on a picnic   b. eat more
   c. lose weight   d. read more books

3. What did the doctor say to Roy?
   a. He is going to be rich.   b. He is going to be poor.
   c. He is going to die soon. d. He is going to be strong.

4. What is NOT true about this story?
   a. Josephine got married to Roy.
   b. Roy tried to lose weight.
   c. Roy lost weight and became a happy man.
   d. Roy is a little boy.

5. How many years did Roy go on a diet?
   a. two years   b. three years
   c. four years   d. five years

Ⓑ **Find the wrong words and cross them out. Then write the correct words.**

After dinner Roy always ate fruits. → sweets

1. Roy couldn't drive a regular car because he was too big. He couldn't sleep in the front seat.   → _____

2. The doctor told Roy, "Now, you need to buy a special house because you're going to die soon."   → _____

3. The doctor told Roy, "You are too small. You have to go on a diet.
                                                → _____

4. Roy went on a picnic.   → _____

LET'S HAVE FUN

Word Puzzle

Across

➡ Across

2. comparative of high
3. comparative of low
6. comparative of long
8. comparative of tall
10. comparative of small

⬇ Down

1. comparative of big
4. comparative of old
5. comparative of short
7. comparative of strong
9. comparative of fast

28

Pantomime

ACTIVITY

studying comparative of adjective by pantomime

things you need : picture cards or word cards

WORD

stronger / bigger / taller / faster / older / longer / shorter / younger / slower / prettier

EXPRESSION

- I am stronger than you.
- I am older than my brother.
- I am faster than her.

A Fill in the blanks. Write the names of your classmates.

1. _____ is big.

2. _____ is bigger.

3. _____ is short.

4. _____ is shorter.

5. _____ is strong.

6. _____ is stronger.

7. _____ is tall.

8. _____ is taller.

9. _____ is old.

10. _____ is older.

B Choose the correct comparative adjective.

1. I am (stronger / more strong) than you.

2. He is (faster / more fast) than you.

3. Nami is (older / more old) than Kevin.

4. This pencil is (longer / more long) than that.

5. The elephant is (bigger / more big) than the fox.

6. This book is (interestinger / more interesting) than that book.

Complete the sentence using the given phrase.

1. _____ is stronger than _____ .

2. _____ is faster than _____ .

3. _____ is shorter than _____ .

4. _____ is taller than _____ .

5. _____ is smarter than _____ .

Listen and fill in the blanks.

Joon : (1)_____ 's my pencil?

Ann : Is this your (2)_____ ?

Joon : No, (3)_____ is (4)_____ than
(5)_____ .

Ann : Is this (6)_____ pencil?

Joon : No, (7)_____ pencil is longer (8)_____
that.

Ann : (9)_____ ! (10)_____ 's your pencil.

PROJECT

Walk around the classroom and ask questions.

Q: Who's stronger / heavier / taller?

Friend's name			

What Do You Want to Do?

1 cook _____
2 birthday _____
3 card _____
4 talk _____
5 dance ___춤추다___
6 play the piano _____
7 sing _____
8 guitar ___기타___

♣ musical _____
♣ show ___쇼___
♣ invite _____
♣ want ___원하다___
♣ make _____
♣ party _____
♣ idea ___아이디어___
♣ tomorrow _____

Look and Listen

Listen and fill in the blanks.

Jenny   : Let's _____ about our show.

           What do you want to do?

Kevin   : Let's _____ .

Mike   : I _____ _____ to sing. I want to dance.

Jenny   : Do you want to _____ ?

           I want to _____ the _____ .

All   : Hwoo ~!

Sam   : I have a good _____ .

All   : _____ do you _____ to _____ ?

Sam   : How about a _____ ?

           We can sing, dance and play the piano.

All   : Sounds good.

Teacher : What do you want to do?

All   : We want to _____ . We want to _____ .

           And we want to _____ the _____ .

Teacher : I know. You want to do a musical.

All   : Yes, that's right.

 # Look at the dialogues and speak in English.

A

우리 같이 노래하자.

난 노래하고 싶지 않아.

너는 뭐 하고 싶은데?

나는 컴퓨터 게임을 하고 싶어.

그래. 좋은 생각이야.

B

내일은 엄마의 생신이야.

너는 엄마를 위해 뭐 하고 싶니?

나는 카드를 만들고 싶어.
너는?

나는 엄마를 위해서
요리를 하고 싶어.

Let's Write

A **Listen to the dialogue again and answer the questions.**

1. What do the students talk about?

2. Does Jenny want to play the violin?

3. What does Jenny want to play?

4. What did the teacher and students decide to do?

5. Does everyone want to dance?

B **Answer these questions about yourself.**

1. Do you like to dance?

2. If you have a show, what would you like to do?

3. What do you usually do for your mom's birthday?

4. Do you cook for your family?

5. What do you often do in your free time?

C **Write in English using "will..."**

1. 나는 내일 피아노를 칠 거야. → _____
2. 나는 영어 공부를 할 거야. → _____
3. 나는 파티를 할 거야. → _____
4. 나는 새 가방을 살 거야. → _____
5. 나는 9시에 잘 거야. → _____

Easy Grammar

Make sentences using the given words.

swim(I)	I want to swim.
	I need to swim.
	I have to swim.

- I / You want to+Verb
- I / You need to+Verb
- I / You have to+Verb
- He / She wants to+Verb
- He / She needs to+Verb
- He /She has to+Verb

1. play soccer(I) _____

_____

_____

2. sing a song(I) _____

_____

_____

3. play the piano(you) _____

_____

_____

4. make a card(she) _____

_____

_____

5. (question) play the guitar(you) _____

_____

_____

What do you Want to do?

Boy 1   Did you finish your homework?

Boy 2   Yes, I did.

Boy 1   Let's go out and play soccer.

Boy 2   No, I don't want to.

Boy 1   Then, what do you want to do?

Boy 2   Umm. How about playing computer games?

Boy 1   Great!

What do you Want to do?

Boy 1   It's boring.

Boy 2   What do you want to do now?

Boy 1   I don't know. Do you have any ideas?

Boy 2   How about playing badminton?

Boy 1   Good! Let's go and play!

LET'S READ

The Birthday Present

Word Bank

look for ~을 찾다

gift 선물

wife 아내

skirt 스커트, 치마

expensive 값비싼

rich 부유한

buy 사다

know 알다

put in 넣다

paper bag 종이 가방

arrive 도착하다

son 아들

snowman 눈사람

put down 내려놓다

garbage truck
쓰레기 트럭

garbage man 환경
미화원

pick up 집다, 줍다

throw 던지다

gone go의 과거분사

remember 기억하다

dump 쓰레기 더미,
쓰레기장

smell 냄새

Poe is looking for a birthday gift for his wife. He sees a pretty skirt. It is expensive. Poe is not rich. But he loves his wife, so he buys the skirt. Poe doesn't want his wife to know about the skirt, so he puts it in a brown paper bag. Then he takes the brown bag to his sister's house.

When Poe arrives at his sister's house, her son is outside making a snowman. "I'll help you," Poe says. He puts the brown paper bag down on the ground. While Poe is making a snowman, a garbage truck comes. The garbage men pick the brown paper bag up and throw it into the truck.

After making the snowman, Poe looks for the brown paper bag. It is gone! Then Poe remembers the garbage truck. So Poe drives to the dump. There are thousands of brown paper bags at the dump. Which one has the skirt? For hours, Poe opens brown paper bags. Finally, he finds the skirt. Poe gives the skirt to his wife on her birthday. "It's beautiful!" she says. "But what is this smell?"

40

A Choose the correct answer.

1. What is the gift for Poe's wife?
   a. a skirt   b. a ring
   c. a jacket   d. a necklace

2. What is the season of the story?
   a. spring   b. summer
   c. fall   d. winter

3. What do the garbage men think that the brown paper bag is?
   a. garbage   b. lunch bag
   c. clothes bag   d. empty bag

4. Why does Poe put his gift in a brown paper bag?
   a. Because he doesn't want to give it to his wife.
   b. Because he wants to change it.
   c. Because he doesn't want his wife to know about it.
   d. Because he likes that brown paper bag.

5. How does his wife feel?
   a. happy   b. angry
   c. sick   d. hungry

B Find the wrong words and cross them out. Then write the correct words.

Poe is looking for a present for his sister. → wife

1. Poe sells the expensive skirt for his wife.   → _____

2. Poe puts the skirt in a blue paper bag.   → _____

3. Poe makes a snowman with his sister's daughter.   → _____

4. The policemen take the brown paper bag to the dump.   → _____

Word Puzzle

* card
* cook
* dance
* good
* guitar
* idea
* invite
* musical
* party
* play
* right
* show
* sing
* soccer
* sound
* talk
* tomorrow
* want

X	X	B	O	P	C	W	Q	S	H	S	F	R	H	D
J	P	I	A	E	J	W	I	T	R	I	T	T	O	K
W	T	A	I	Y	O	N	Z	H	V	N	P	N	O	W
Y	D	M	R	H	G	Z	J	G	R	G	I	O	P	T
C	R	N	S	T	Y	W	R	I	B	I	C	J	O	W
G	R	A	U	K	Y	A	A	R	K	B	L	M	K	L
S	A	E	T	O	O	Z	L	N	X	W	O	A	A	P
C	P	E	C	I	S	V	M	P	T	R	I	C	W	F
I	D	S	D	C	U	O	M	W	R	Z	I	T	E	N
Z	A	O	Z	I	O	G	D	O	N	S	C	T	G	K
W	I	U	O	U	Y	S	W	Y	U	Q	I	D	D	U
X	V	J	N	G	K	E	V	M	A	V	O	R	K	K
R	J	L	F	R	M	Z	N	E	N	D	A	N	C	E
F	Y	D	E	N	X	S	H	I	K	C	J	B	S	S
T	B	W	U	W	T	B	N	M	I	D	T	A	L	K

42

Chinese Whisper

ACTIVITY

speaking a sentence in a whisper
things you need : a set of picture card

WORD

sing / dance / play / musical / want / jump / run / swim / study / visit / make / cook
/ throw / run

EXPRESSION

- I want to sing a song.
- I want to dance.
- I want to play the violin.

A Write in English.

1. 나는 영화를 볼 것이다. → _____.

2. 나는 쇼핑을 갈 것이다. → _____.

3. 그녀는 자전거를 탈 것이다. → _____.

4. 우리는 여행을 갈 것이다. → _____.

5. 그들은 내일 서울에 올 것이다. → _____.

6. 나는 피아노를 칠 것이다. → _____.

7. 그들은 골프를 칠 것이다. → _____.

8. 우리는 축구를 할 것이다. → _____.

9. 그는 중고차(used car)를 살 것이다. → _____.

10. 그녀는 새 드레스를 살 것이다. → _____.

B Write in correct order.

1. I / . / to / sing / want

_____

2. I / the / guitar / play / . / want / to

_____

3. ? / How / you / about

_____

4. invite / to / I / want / friends / . / my

_____

5. a / party / I / . / to / want / have

_____

C Choose the correct answer.

1. Let's talk _____ our show.

   a. to   b. with   c. for   d. about

2. I _____ a good idea.

   a. take   b. have   c. put   d. meet

3. I want to cook _____ mom.

   a. to   b. between   c. for   d. about

4. Can you join _____?

   a. we   b. our   c. us   d. ours

5. _____ do you want to do?

   a. What   b. Where   c. Who   d. Whom

D Listen and fill in the blanks.

Namsu : (1)_____ is (2)_____ 's birthday.

Nami : (3)_____ do you (4)_____ to
(5)_____ for mom?

Namsu : I (6)_____ to (7)_____ a (8)_____.
(9)_____ about you?

Nami : I want to (10)_____ for mom.

PROJECT

Now, you have a great servant Ginny who does everything you want. You just give him a wish.

Q: Let's ask your friends what he or she wants to wish. I want to...

Friend's name   **Wish**

Will You Help Me, Please?

❶ heavy _____

❷ bucket _____

❸ move 움직이다, 옮기다

❹ hold _____

❺ paint _____

❻ painting _____

❼ tired 피곤한

❽ paper _____

❾ airplane _____

♣ pass _____

♣ help 돕다

♣ will _____

♣ problem _____

♣ together _____

Look and Listen

Listen and fill in the blanks.

Mom : _____ you help me, honey?

Dad : _____ _____.

Nami : Dad, will you help me _____ _____ _____,
       please?

Dad : Of course.

Namsu : Will you help me, dad?

Dad : Ha, ha, sure! _____ the _____?

Mom : Honey! _____ you _____ _____?

Dad : OK!

Namsu : Dad, will you help me, please?
Nami

Dad : _____ _____.

_____ _____ _____.

Namsu : Dad~!
Nami

Dad : I'm coming.

48

Look and Speak

 Look at the dialogues and speak in English.

A

저 좀 도와줄래요?

물론이지요. 뭐가 문제예요?

이 테이블이 너무 무거워요. 같이 옮겨요.

물론이에요.

B

종이 좀 건네줄래?

물론이지. 뭐 하고 싶은데?

비행기를 만들고 싶어. 나 좀 도와줄래?

물론이지.

고마워.

천만에.

Let's Write

A **Listen to the dialogue again and answer the questions.**

1. What does Nami ask to her father?

2. Why does mother ask father to carry the flowerpot?

3. What does father say?

4. Is father tired?

5. What do they say to their father to ask something?

B **Answer these questions using "I have to…"**

1. What do you have to do before your meal?

2. What do you have to do if you have a test tomorrow?

3. What do you have to do when you are sick?

4. What do you have to do if your bike is broken?

5. What do you have to do before you go to bed?

C **Write in English.**

1. 그들은 일찍 일어나야 한다.   →

2. 우리는 학교에 가야 한다.   →

3. 난 엄마를 도와야 한다.   →

4. 그녀는 피아노를 연주해야 한다.   →

Easy Grammar

Make sentences using the given words.

help me	→	Will you help me?
my homework	→	Will you help me with my homework?
the salt	→	Will you pass me the salt?

- Will you+Verb ~?
- Will you help me with+Noun ~?
- Will you pass me+Noun ~?

1. the paper   → _____

2. the sugar   → _____

3. taste this soup   → _____

4. taste this *Kimchi*   → _____

5. turn on the TV   → _____

6. turn it off   → _____

7. open your book   → _____

8. make sandwiches for me

                        → _____

9. wash this potato   → _____

The Merry-Go-Round

The mer-ry-go-round goes round and round. The child - ren laughed and laughed and laughed. So ma - ny were go - ing round and round that the mer - ry - go - round col - lapsed.

Will you help me?

Jack   Hi, Tom. What are you doing?

Tom   I'm painting this.

Jack   Is it fun?

Tom   Will you help me, please?

Jack   Of course. I like painting.

Tom   Good.

Dad   Where are you going, Tom?

Tom   Oh, no.

Dad   Oh, Jack! You are a good boy!

Jack   Thank you.

Dad   Tom, please help your friend, Jack.
Will you hold the bucket?

Tom   ?????

The Coin

Word Bank

December 12월

bake 빵을 굽다

dessert 후식, 디저트

put into ~에 넣다

coin 동전

luck 행운

find 발견하다

put on ~에 올려놓다

fourth 네 번째

missing 없어진, 사라진

realize 깨닫다

cough 기침하다

grow up 자라다

get married 결혼하다

sore throat 목 아픔

It was December 25. Mike, a 13-year-old American boy, was happy. His mother was baking a special pie for dessert. His mother put four small coins into the pie. The four coins were for good luck. After dinner Mike and his family ate the pie. They found three coins in the pie and put them on the sink. Where was the fourth coin? It was missing, but Mike's mother didn't realize. After Christmas, Mike got sick. He coughed, and he couldn't say anything. Mike's parents took him to the hospital. The doctors said, "We have no ideas."

For 10 years Mike didn't speak. He grew up, and he got married. But he never spoke.

One day, when Mike was 26 years old, he got a sore throat at home. He began to cough. He coughed up something black. He took it to the hospital. A doctor at the hospital said, "This is a coin! I think you can speak again." Soon Mike was talking.

A Choose the correct answer.

1. Mike's mother put four small _____ in her pie.
   a. dried grapes   b. coins
   c. nuts   d. toys

2. There were only three coins on the sink. Where was the fourth coin? It was
   _____.
   a. in Mike's pocket   b. in Mike's drawer
   c. in Mike's stomach   d. in Mike's bag

3. One coin was missing, but Mike's mother didn't pay attention. She didn't
   _____ that the coin was missing.
   a. cook   b. make
   c. realize   d. find

4. Mike got sick. He _____, and he couldn't speak.
   a. cried   b. shouted
   c. coughed   d. ate

5. When Mike was 26 years old, he coughed up _____.
   a. a candy   b. a marble
   c. a cherry   d. a coin

B Find the wrong words and cross them out. Then write the correct words.

Mike, a 13-year-old ~~French~~ boy, was happy. → American

1. His mother was making a special chocolate for dessert.   → _____

2. Mike's mother put four small marbles into the pie for good luck. → _____

3. After breakfast Mike and his family ate the pie.   → _____

4. They found three coins in the pie and put them on the floor.   → _____

LET'S HAVE FUN

Word Puzzle

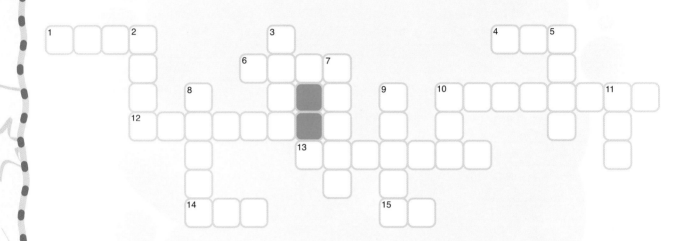

→ **Across**

1. Will you ( ) this potato?

4. I have to go ( ).

6. Please ( ) me the paper.

10. Let's move it ( ).

12. Will you help me,( )?

13. What's the ( )?

14. Will ( ) help me with my homework?

15. I have ( ) clean this bike.

↓ **Down**

2. Will you ( ) me, honey?

3. I want to ( ) an airplane.

5. Will you help me ( ) my homework?

7. ( ), I can't help you because...

8. This table is too ( ).

9. I want to make a ( ).

10. Will you pass me ( ) book?

11. I want to ( ) a sandwich.

Problem Solving

ACTIVITY

matching two sentences with the same meaning

things you need : situation cards and solution cards

WORD

help / sorry / No problem / Of course / homework / heavy / clean /
Thank you / You're welcome

EXPRESSION

- Will you help me with my homework?
- Will you help me with my study?
- Will you help me with this problem?

Test Yourself!

A. Write in English using "have / has to..." or "don't / doesn't have to..."

1. 나는 선생님을 도와드려야 한다. → _____

2. 우리는 일찍 일어나야 한다. → _____

3. 학생들은 책을 많이 읽어야 한다. → _____

4. 그들은 청소를 해야 한다. → _____

5. 엄마는 파티를 준비해야(prepare) 한다. → _____

6. 나는 양치질을 해야 한다. → _____

7. 그녀는 요리를 해야 한다. → _____

8. 나는 일찍 일어날 필요가 없다. → _____

9. 너는 학교에 갈 필요가 없다. → _____

10. 나는 형을 도울 필요가 없다. → _____

B. Match the sentences.

1. Will you help me? •   • a. Get some rest.

2. This table is too heavy. •   • b. Of course.

3. I am so tired. •   • c. I am going home.

4. Thank you very much. •   • d. Let's move it together.

5. Where are you going? •   • e. You're welcome.

Choose the correct answer.

1. What are you _____ ?

   a. doing   b. do   c. done   d. to do

2. What do you want _____ ?

   a. to eat   b. eat   c. eating   d. eaten

3. Will you help me _____ my homework?

   a. to   b. with   c. for   d. about

4. _____ you pass me the salt?

   a. Must   b. Have   c. Do   d. Will

5. I want to make _____ airplane.

   a. an   b. a   c. two   d. many

Listen and fill in the blanks.

Nami : Please, (1)_____ me the (2)_____ .

Namsu : (3)_____ . What do you want to do?

Nami : I want to (4)_____ an (5)_____ .

    (6)_____ you (7)_____ me?

Namsu : No (8)_____ .

Nami : (9)_____ you.

Namsu : You're (10)_____ .

PROJECT

List 10 things you have to do before school and after school.

Before school, I have to...

After school, I have to...

That's Too Bad

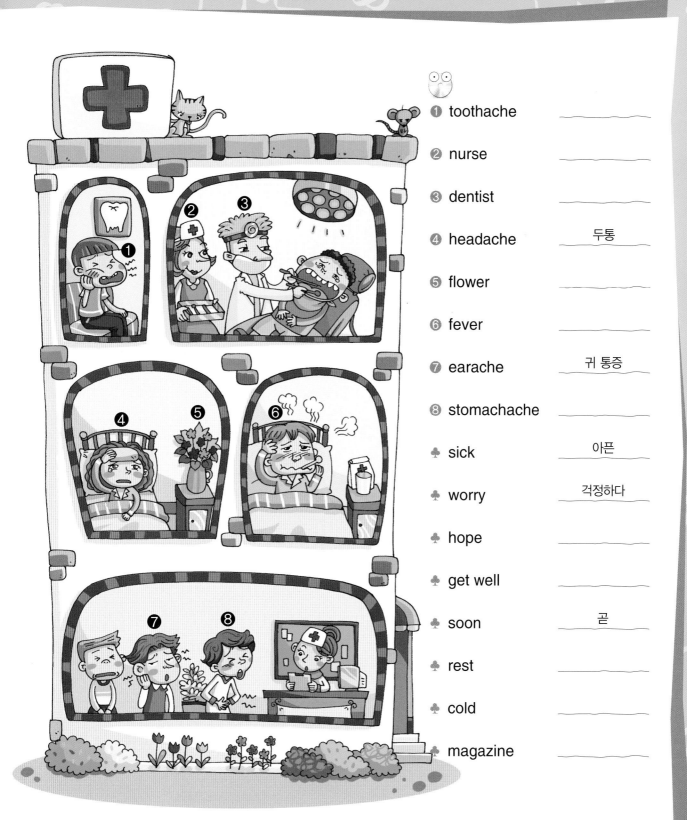

1. toothache _____
2. nurse _____
3. dentist _____
4. headache _____ 두통
5. flower _____
6. fever _____
7. earache _____ 귀 통증
8. stomachache _____
♣ sick _____ 아픈
♣ worry _____ 걱정하다
♣ hope _____
♣ get well _____
♣ soon _____ 곧
♣ rest _____
♣ cold _____
♣ magazine _____

Look and Listen

Listen and fill in the blanks.

Teacher : Hello, Mrs. Brown _____.

Mom : Hi, Mrs. Brown. This is Kevin's mom.

Teacher : Oh, Mrs. Park. How are you?

Mom : Fine, thanks. Ummm.

Mrs. Brown, Kevin _____ go to _____

today.

Teacher : Why?

Mom : Because he's sick. He has a _____ _____.

Teacher : That's _____ _____.

Mom : Don't _____, Mrs. Brown.

He will be OK soon.

Teacher : I _____ so.

Children : Hi, Kevin. How are you?

Kevin : I'm OK.

Children : This is _____ _____.

Kevin : Thank you very much.

62

Look and Speak

Look at the dialogues and speak in English.

A

우리 오늘 오후에 축구하자.

미안해. 난 못해.

왜?

왜냐하면 내가 아프거든.
머리가 아파.

오, 안됐구나. 좀 쉬도록 해.

응. 그럴 거야.

B

여보세요? 저는 앤입니다.

안녕, 앤. 나는 메리 고모란다.

안녕하세요, 메리 고모님. 잘 지내시나요?

나는 잘 지내고 있단다.
너는 어떠니?

저는 잘 지내요.
그런데 엄마가 배가 아프세요.

저런 안됐구나.

Let's Write

A Listen to the dialogue again and answer the questions.

1. What does Kevin's mom say?

_____

2. What is the problem with Kevin?

_____

3. What do friends do for Kevin?

_____

4. Does Kevin feel better with friends?

_____

B Answer these questions about yourself.

1. What do you do if you have a headache?

_____

2. How do you feel today?

_____

3. What is the first thing you do when you have a bad cold?

_____

4. Do you have a cavity?

_____

5. Do you like going to the hospital?

_____

C Write in English.

1. 난 두통이 있어.   → _____

2. 빨리 회복되기를 바래. → _____

3. 난 치통이 있어.   → _____

4. 무슨 일이니?   → _____

5. 정말 안됐구나.   → _____

 Easy Grammar

Make sentences using the given words.

Ann	Hello. This is Ann speaking.
Aunt Mary	Hello, Ann. This is Aunt Mary.
Ann	How are you?
Aunt Mary(stomachache)	I have a stomachache.

- This is ~
  =This is ~
  speaking
- I have a/an ~

1. Bill _____

   Uncle Kim _____

   Bill How are you?

   Uncle Kim(headache) _____

2. Tom _____

   Michelle _____

   Tom How are you?

   Michelle(sore throat) _____

3. Jim _____

   Grandfather _____

   Jim How are you?

   Grandfather(toothache) _____

4. Amy _____

   Grandmother _____

   Amy How are you?

   Grandmother(earache) _____

Skidama Rinka Dinka Dink

Why don't you go see a doctor?

Boy	You don't look well. Are you okay?
Girl	I'm sick now. I have a bad cold.
Boy	That's too bad. Why don't you go see a doctor?
Girl	I'm going to the hospital now.
Boy	I hope you'll get better soon.
Girl	Thank you.

Take some medicine

Girl	Let's go out and play.
Boy	Sorry, I can't.
Girl	What's wrong with you?
Boy	I have a stomachache.
Girl	That's too bad. Take some medicine.
Boy	OK. I will.

Man's Best Friend

Word Bank

once upon a time 옛날에

like to ~하기를 좋아하다

take a walk 산책하다

next to ~ 옆에

simple 단순한

life 생명, 목숨, 삶

spring 봄

die 죽다

bury 묻다

cemetery 묘지

grave 무덤

cry 울다

leave 떠나다

weather 날씨

ground 땅바닥

finally 마침내

Once upon a time, in a small house in England, two friends lived together. Their names were Rohn and Tobby. Rohn and Tobby were not rich, but they were happy. Rohn and Tobby liked to take long walks together. After their walk, Rohn and Tobby had dinner next to the fire. They had a simple but happy life.

In the spring of 1868, Rohn died. He was buried in a cemetery. After Rohn was buried, Tobby stood at Rohn's grave and cried. For the next 12 years, Tobby never left the cemetery. When the weather was bad, he slept in a small house at the cemetery. When the weather was good, he slept on the ground next to Rohn's grave. Finally, in 1882, Tobby died, too. Friends buried him in a little grave next to Rohn. Why was Tobby's grave little? Tobby was a little dog.

68

A Choose the correct answer.

1. Where did the story take place?
   a. Australia   b. Japan
   c. England   d. France

2. How many years did Tobby stay at the cemetery for?
   a. nine years   b. ten years
   c. eleven years   d. twelve years

3. Rohn and Tobby were _____.
   a. runners   b. brothers
   c. cousins   d. an owner and a pet

4. Why was the grave for Tobby small?
   a. Because Tobby was a little baby.
   b. Because Tobby was a little dog.
   c. Because Tobby liked something small.
   d. Because there was not enough space.

5. When did Tobby die?
   a. in 1868   b. in 1880
   c. in 1882   d. in 1886

B Find the wrong words and cross them out. Then write the correct words.

Two friends lived together in a ~~big~~ house. → small

1. Their names were John and Sammy   → _____

2. In the summer of 1868, Rohn died.   → _____

3. Tobby stood at Rohn's bed and cried.   → _____

4. Tobby lived in the cemetery for four years. → _____

LET'S HAVE FUN

Word Puzzle

* after
* aunt
* bad
* because
* cloudy
* earache
* fine
* fun
* great
* hope
* how
* present
* rest
* sick
* soon
* speaking
* stomachache
* toothache
* worry

W	M	W	O	H	H	C	O	A	W	O	B	L	P	J
E	E	X	E	T	K	H	T	O	E	S	Y	E	Y	V
S	N	H	W	S	N	C	I	A	M	N	H	R	R	P
U	I	Z	C	M	L	U	I	W	E	C	I	V	R	S
A	Z	K	Y	A	R	E	A	S	A	R	A	F	O	C
C	O	A	R	I	H	Z	L	H	O	D	G	S	W	E
E	T	Z	U	Q	W	C	T	U	C	Z	H	K	M	A
B	R	Q	Z	W	X	O	A	P	I	S	W	S	T	R
W	U	L	O	G	O	I	H	M	R	L	P	X	R	A
C	F	Z	I	T	Y	X	J	C	O	E	E	P	G	C
L	U	L	W	W	A	D	A	B	A	T	S	P	N	H
O	N	D	N	F	S	T	R	K	Z	V	S	E	O	E
U	W	I	T	O	K	U	I	E	H	Y	G	G	N	H
D	G	E	O	T	R	N	W	R	S	H	O	P	F	T
Y	R	N	I	R	G	I	W	P	I	T	I	V	R	C

Simon says

ACTIVITY

saying the problem you have using "Simon says..." and repeating what you hear

WORD

stomachache / headache / backache / toothache / fever / sore throat / cough / cold / earache

EXPRESSION

- I have a stomachache.
- I have a bad cold.
- I have a cough.

Simon says,

A Write in English.

1. 난 배가 아파. → _____

2. 난 감기 걸렸어. → _____

3. 그는 치통이 있어. → _____

4. 그녀는 기침을 해. → _____

5. 빨리 회복하길 바래. → _____

6. 너 몸이 아프니? → _____

7. 난 약을 먹었어. → _____

8. 감기 걸렸니? → _____

9. 기분은 좋아졌니? → _____

10. 난 귀가 아파. → _____

B Write in correct order.

1. Hello / , / speaking / . / Mrs. / Brown

_____

2. has / He / . / cold / bad / a

_____

3. Thank / much / . / very / you

_____

4. Let's / this / afternoon / . / soccer / play

_____

5. it / going / ? / How / is

_____

C Choose the correct answer.

1. I am _____ happy today.

   a. to   b. too   c. soon   d. so

2. That's _____ bad.

   a. to   b. too   c. two   d. much

3. She must do _____ homework.

   a. her   b. he   c. his   d. hers

4. This is Ann _____ .

   a. speak   b. to speak   c. spoken   d. speaking

5. _____ do you want to go?

   a. What   b. Where   c. Who   d. Whom

D Listen and fill in the blanks.

Ann   : Hello. (1)_____ is Ann (2)_____ .

Aunt Mary : (3)_____ , Ann. This is aunt Mary.

Ann   : Hi, (4)_____ Mary. (5)_____ are you?

Aunt Mary : I'm (6)_____ . How (7)_____ you?

Ann   : I'm (8)_____ , but mom has a (9)_____ .

Aunt Mary : Oh, that's too (10)_____ .

PROJECT

Q: What do you usually do when you have a bad cold and a headache?

for a bad cold

for a headache

74

Would You Like to Come to My House?

❶ prince	_____		♣ delicious	맛있는	
❷ eat	_____		♣ invite	_____	
❸ put on	_____		♣ join	합치다, 함께하다	
❹ fox	_____		♣ write	_____	
❺ take off	(옷, 신발을) 벗다		♣ wear	_____	
❻ turkey	칠면조		♣ try	_____	
❼ pie	_____		♣ model	_____	
❽ snake	_____		♣ from	~로부터	
♣ Thanksgiving Day	추수감사절				

Look and Listen

Listen and fill in the blanks.

Ann : This _____ is Thanksgiving Day.

Nami : Thanksgiving Day?

Ann : Yes. Would you like to _____ to my _____?

Nami : Yes, I'd love to.

Jinho : Sounds good.

Ann : Welcome! Come in!

Nami, Jinho : Thanks.

Ann : Oh, don't _____ _____ your shoes.

　　　　We don't take off our _____ in the house.

Nami, Jinho : Oh, I see.

Jinho : What's that? Is it _____?

Ann : No. That's _____.

　　　　We eat turkey on _____ Day.

Ann's Dad : Try it.

Ann's Mom : Would you like to _____ this pie?

Nami, Ann, Jinho : Woo!

Nami : Oh, it looks _____.

76

Look and Speak

Look at the dialogues and speak in English.

A

뭐 하고 있니?

모형 비행기를 만들고 있어.

재미있니?

물론이지.
너도 같이 할래?

그래, 하고 싶어.

B

어서 와!

초대해 줘서 고마워.

코트 벗어도 돼.

고마워.

신발은 벗지 마.
우리는 집에서 신발을 신어.

오우, 그렇구나.

 Let's Write

A **Listen to the dialogue again and answer the questions.**

    1. What holiday is it?   _____

    2. What do Nami and Jinho do when they get in the house?

               _____

    3. What special food do they eat?   _____

    4. Do they like that food?   _____

    5. Are they wearing shoes in the house? _____

B **Answer these questions.**

    1. What would you like to do for this Christmas?

        _____

    2. What would you like to have for a Christmas gift?

        _____

    3. What would you like to do this Sunday?

        _____

    4. Where would you like to go?

        _____

    5. Who would you like to meet?

        _____

C **Write in English using "I'd like to…"**

    1. 나는 저녁으로 스테이크를 먹고 싶어. → _____

    2. 나는 영화를 보고 싶어. → _____

    3. 나는 일본에 가 보고 싶어. → _____

    4. 나는 파티를 하고 싶어. → _____

    5. 나는 재미있는 책을 읽고 싶어. → _____

 Easy Grammar

Make the sentences using the given words.

come to my house	Would you like to come to my house?
come to my school	Would you like to come to my school?
come to her school	Would you like to come to her school?

Would you like to+
Verb ~?

1. come to her house _____

2. go camping with me _____

3. have lunch with me _____

4. go fishing with me _____

5. come to my birthday party _____

6. try this turkey _____

7. try this pie _____

8. sing a song _____

9. eat some apples _____

Little Prince

Little Prince	Hi, I'm a little prince.
Snake	Hi, I'm a snake.
Little Prince	My birthday is this Thursday.
Snake	Thursday?
Little Prince	Would you like to come to my house?
Snake	Sorry, I can't.
Little Prince	Hi, I'm a little prince.
Fox	Hi, I'm a fox. Where are you from?
Little Prince	I'm from up there. My birthday is this Thursday.
Fox	Birthday?
Little Prince	Would you like to come to my house?
Fox	Sure.
Little Prince	Thank you.

LET'S READ

Lost and Found

Word Bank

understand 이해하다

call 부르다

easy 쉬운

explain 설명하다

before ~전에

address 주소

believe 믿다

same 같은

curly 곱슬머리의

be adopted 입양되다

find out 발견하다

twins 쌍둥이

be born 태어나다

newspaper 신문

triplets 세 쌍둥이

Rob was happy at a school. But Rob didn't understand when some students said "Hi, Teddy!" to him. He asked his friend, "Why do some students call me Teddy?" "Oh, that's easy to explain," the boy said. "Teddy was a student here before. You look like Teddy." Rob wanted to see Teddy. He got Teddy's address from a friend and Rob couldn't believe his eyes. Rob and Teddy had the same color eyes and same smile. They had the same brown, curly hair. They also had the same birthday. And they both were adopted.

Rob and Teddy found out that they were twins. Soon after they were born, one family adopted Rob, and another family adopted Teddy.

Rob and Teddy's story was in the newspaper. There was a photo of Rob and Teddy next to the story. A young man named Dave saw the photo in the newspaper. Dave couldn't believe his eyes. He had the same color eyes and the same smile. He had the same brown, curly hair. He had the same birthday. And he, too, was adopted.

Later Dave met Rob and Teddy. When Rob and Teddy saw Dave, they couldn't believe their eyes. Rob, Teddy, and Dave are triplets.

A Choose the correct answer.

1. What is the other name friends called Rob?
   a. Teddy   b. Harry
   c. Steve   d. Bob

2. What does Rob look like?
   a. black straight hair   b. brown curly hair
   c. short dark brown hair   d. blond curly hair

3. Where did Dave see the picture of Rob and Teddy?
   a. in the newspaper   b. in the magazine
   c. in the school paper   d. on TV

4. What is true about Rob, Teddy and Dave?
   a. They are not brothers.   b. They are triplets.
   c. They go to same school.   d. They never meet one another.

5. What is NOT true about Rob, Teddy and Dave?
   a. They have the same color eyes.   b. They were adopted.
   c. They have the same birthday.   d. They live with their real mom and dad.

B Find the wrong words and cross them out. Then write the correct words.

Teddy was a student here before. Now he goes to another ~~town~~. → school

1. Rob and Teddy's story was in the storybook.   → _____

2. Rob and Teddy had the same color eyes and the same shapes. → _____

3. Dave looked exactly different from Rob and Teddy!   → _____

Word Puzzle

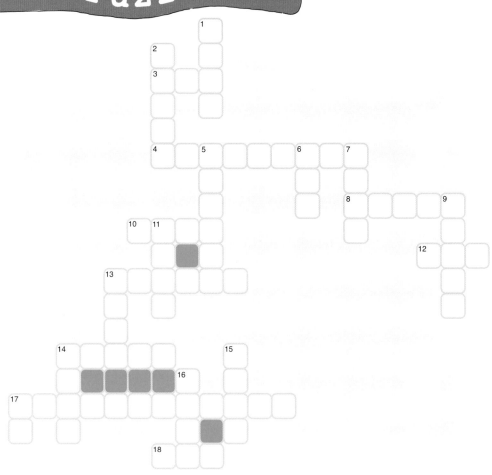

→ Across

3. We don't take off (   ) shoes in the house.
4. Oh, it looks (   ).
8. We're making a (   ) plane.
10. (   ) are you doing?
12. Thank you (   ) inviting me.
13. We eat (   ) on Thanksgiving Day.
14. (   ) are you from?
17. This Thursday is (   ) Day.
18. Oh, I (   ).

↓ Down

1. I will do my home(   ) after school.
2. (   ) you like to come to my house?
5. Hi, I'm a (   ) prince.
6. Oh, don't take (   ) your shoes.
7. Would you like to have (   ) juice?
9. Oh, it (   ) delicious.
11. Please write your name (   ).
13. Oh, don't (   ) off your shoes.
14. We (   ) our shoes in the house.
15. Would you like to (   ) us?
16. Would you (   ) to come to my house?
17. Would you like to come (   ) my house?

Word Chain

ACTIVITY
connecting last word in English

WORD

all the words that you know

EXPRESSION
• make them any sentences freely

A Fill in the blanks with the right words.

1. My mom would like to _____ steak for dinner.

2. I would like to _____ my uncle in London.

3. They would like to _____ a big party tonight.

4. He would like to _____ a movie *"Harry Porter."*

5. She would like to _____ a beautiful dress.

B Write in English using "would like to..."

1. 나는 친구들을 많이 초대하고 싶어.

→ _____

2. 샐러드와 스테이크를 먹고 싶어.

→ _____

3. 너 주스 좀 마실래?

→ _____

4. 영화 보러 갈래?

→ _____

5. 나는 곰인형(teddy bear)을 갖고 싶어.

→ _____

C Find the opposite word and match them.

1. come •   • a. that

2. fun •   • b. bad

3. little •   • c. boring

4. good •   • d. go

5. this •   • e. big

D Choose the correct answer.

1. _____ you like to come to my house?

   a. Can   b. Would   c. Will   d. Are

2. Don't take _____ your shoes.

   a. on   b. off   c. from   d. for

3. Thank you _____ inviting me.

   a. to   b. with   c. for   d. about

4. Where are you _____?

   a. on   b. by   c. from   d. for

5. I will _____ a birthday party.

   a. have   b. meet   c. go   d. play

E Listen and fill in the blanks.

Ann : (1)_____!

Nami : Thank you for (2)_____ me.

Ann : You can take (3)_____ your (4)_____.

Nami : (5)_____.

Ann : Oh, (6)_____ take off your (7)_____.

        We (8)_____ our shoes in the (9)_____.

Nami : Oh, I (10)_____.

PROJECT

Walk around the classroom and ask questions.

Q: What would your classmates like to have and do for their birthday?

Friend's name	would like to have...	would like to do...

It's Time to Go Home

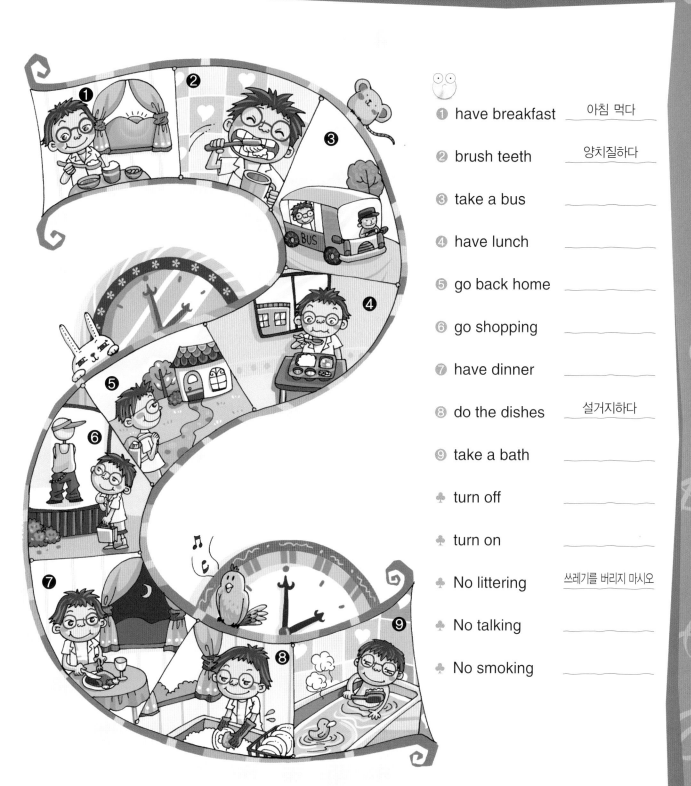

1 have breakfast — 아침 먹다

2 brush teeth — 양치질하다

3 take a bus — _____

4 have lunch — _____

5 go back home — _____

6 go shopping — _____

7 have dinner — _____

8 do the dishes — 설거지하다

9 take a bath — _____

♣ turn off — _____

♣ turn on — _____

♣ No littering — 쓰레기를 버리지 마시오

♣ No talking — _____

♣ No smoking — _____

Look and Listen

Listen and fill in the blanks.

Dad　: Let's _____ _____.

Nami : Wow! Great!

Mom　: I _____ skate _____.

Dad　: Come on. I'll help you.

Mom　: Where's Nami?

Dad　: She's _____ there. She is a good _____.

Mom　: Nami. Don't go that way. _____ _____!

　　　　Nami, come here. It's _____ _____ go home.

Nami : What time is it?

Mom　: It's _____ already. Let's _____ _____.

Nami : Not now. I want to _____ _____.

Mom　: _____ _____, Nami.

Dad　: Oh, no.

90

Look and Speak

Look at the dialogues and speak in English.

A

자, 이제 설거지를 할 시간이다.

누구 차례지?

전 아니에요.
남수 차례예요.

알고 있어.

B

남수야, 숙제 할 시간이야.

TV 먼저 봐도 될까요?

안 돼. 숙제 먼저 해라.
지금은 TV 보지 마.

알겠어요.

Let's Write

A **Listen to the dialogue again and answer the questions.**

1. Where are they? _____

2. Can Nami's mom skate well? _____

3. Who is a good skater? _____

4. Who can help mom skate? _____

5. What time is it now? _____

B **Answer these questions about yourself.**

1. What time do you usually wake up?

_____

2. What do you do first in the morning?

_____

3. What do you do before dinner?

_____

4. What are you going to do today after school?

_____

5. What do you usually do after dinner?

_____

C **Write in English.**

1. 학교 갈 시간이야. → _____

2. 벌써 7시야. 집에 갈 시간이야. → _____

3. 기차 탈 시간이야. → _____

4. 숙제 할 시간이야. 텔레비전 꺼라. → _____

5. 너무 늦었어. 잘 시간이야. → _____

Easy Grammar

Make proper answers to the time.

> It's time to get up.   Don't sleep too much.
> It's time to have breakfast.   Don't eat cookies.
> It's time to go to school.   Don't be late.

- play soccer too long
- watch TV too much
- go out
- stay up late
- eat candies
- be lazy

1. It's time to go back home.

_____

2. It's time to do your homework.

_____

3. It's time to do the dishes.

_____

4. It's time to go to bed.

_____

5. It's time to brush your teeth.

_____

6. It's time to study for the test.

_____

Hickory Dickory Dock

It's time to study

Girl   What are you doing now?

Boy   I'm watching TV now.

Girl   Come on. Turn it off. It's time to study!

Boy   Wait a minute, please.

Girl   No, study for the test now!

Boy   OK.

Girl   Mom   Boy   Son

It's time to go to bed!

Boy 1   Where are you?

Boy 2   I'm here in my bedroom reading a book.

Boy 1   Isn't it time to go to bed?

Boy 2   I want to finish reading this book.

Boy 1   No, it's too late.

Boy 2   OK.

Boy 1   Dad   Boy 2   Son

Thanks a Million

Word Bank

give 주다

other 다른

people 사람들

poor 가난한

hard 열심히

businessman 사업가

remember 기억하다

send 보내다

letter 편지

secretary 비서

read 읽다

decide 결심하다

usually 보통, 대개

from time to time 이따금

hearing aid 보청기

washing machine 세탁기

healthy 건강한

mad 미친, 화난

gone 사라진

million 백만

Berry Loss was a rich man. But he gave it all to other people. When he was little, he was very poor. He worked very hard and became a rich businessman. But he remembered the time when he was poor. He wanted to help poor people.

How did Mr. Loss give people money? People send him letters. Mr. Loss and his secretaries read all the letters. Then Mr. Loss decided to give money to some people.

He usually sent money to old people, sick people, and poor children.

From time to time, Mr. Loss didn't give people money. He sent them things they wanted – shoes, a bike, a watch, a hearing aid, new bottles and pans, or a washing machine.

Mr. Loss mostly didn't send money to young, healthy people. Some people were mad when Mr. Loss didn't send them money.

For twenty one years, Berry Loss gave money to people. Then, in 2000, he stopped. Why? All his money was gone. "I gave $30 million away," he said. "That's all I had. Now I have no money. But in many ways, I am a rich man."

A Choose the correct answer.

1. How did Mr. Loss spend all his money?
   a. to buy an expensive car   b. to build a big house
   c. to travel around the world   d. to help poor people

2. Who could get money from Mr. Loss?
   a. good looking boys   b. kind teachers
   c. poor people   d. beautiful ladies

3. Who couldn't get money from Mr. Loss?
   a. poor people   b. sick people
   c. old people   d. young people

4. Why were some people mad at Mr. Loss?
   a. Because they couldn't get money.   b. Because they get too much money.
   c. Because Mr. Loss is not kind.   d. Because Mr. Loss is very selfish.

5. What does Mr. Loss think about himself?
   a. He is a poor man.   b. He is a lucky man.
   c. He is a rich man.   d. He is a wise man.

B Find the wrong words and cross them out. Then write the correct words.

When Mr. Loss was a little boy, he was ~~rich~~. → <u>poor</u>

1. Mr. Loss worked hard and became a successful lawyer.   → _____

2. Mr. Loss wanted to give some of his money away.

                                                                 → _____

3. Mr. Loss usually sent money to old people, healthy people, and poor children.

                                                                 → _____

4. Some people were happy when Mr. Loss didn't send them money.

                                                                 → _____

Word Puzzle

* already
* back
* bed
* breakfast
* computer
* cookies
* dinner
* dishes
* get-up
* home
* homework
* late
* look
* lunch
* much
* over
* see
* skate
* ski
* soccer
* time
* turn
* watch
* watch-out

O	C	K	S	K	A	T	E	X	Y	B	H	B	F	M
E	R	T	J	N	S	K	N	Y	E	W	A	T	C	H
Y	E	T	S	F	K	E	O	D	G	E	K	H	F	C
A	T	Q	U	A	E	A	M	O	D	L	K	D	C	N
R	U	K	P	O	F	E	T	O	L	I	A	J	R	U
E	P	H	R	R	-	K	S	D	H	X	S	T	G	L
N	M	R	M	O	A	H	A	R	T	V	X	H	E	M
N	O	U	N	N	W	I	C	E	T	I	M	E	E	A
I	C	A	U	A	M	E	Q	T	R	F	E	R	K	S
D	N	L	P	K	Q	I	M	W	A	B	Y	E	Z	M
H	R	R	W	B	Z	S	K	O	D	W	Q	V	Y	U
N	U	E	R	O	K	X	A	S	H	Q	B	O	U	C
G	T	A	T	X	C	S	R	P	U	-	T	E	G	H
T	I	D	G	I	A	S	O	C	C	E	R	L	M	P
C	E	Y	N	P	B	S	E	I	K	O	O	C	R	C

Bingo Game

ACTIVITY

studying time and activities through bingo game
things you need : bingo tables as many as the students

WORD

time / get up / breakfast / lunch / homework / dishes / go shopping /
already / put on / away / sleep / yet

EXPRESSION

- I get up at 7:00.
- I have breakfast at 7:30.
- I go to school at 8:00.
- I have lunch at 12:00.

A Write in English.

1. 영어 공부할 시간이야. → _____

2. 아침 식사 시간이야. → _____

3. 학교 갈 시간이야. → _____

4. 교실에서 뛰지 마! → _____

5. 영어 시간에 한국말 하지 마! → _____

6. 그 쓰레기 주워! → _____

7. 가지 마! → _____

8. 주차금지 → _____

9. 금연 → _____

10. 음식물 반입 금지 → _____

B Write in correct order.

1. time / ? / What / it / is

   → _____

2. there / is / She / . /over

   → _____

3. time / dishes / the / . / It's / to / do

   → _____

4. Can / computer / I / ? / play / games

   → _____

5. time / go / to / . / It's / to / school

   → _____

C Choose the correct answer.

1. She is a good _____ .

   a. skate   b. skater   c. skates   d. skating

2. It's time to _____ your homework.

   a. take   b. have   c. put   d. do

3. It's time to _____ the dishes.

   a. take   b. have   c. put   d. do

4. I get up _____ 6 o'clock.

   a. on   b. off   c. at   d. for

5. I go to _____ bed at 10 o'clock.

   a. a   b. an   c. for   d. 없음

D Listen and fill in the blanks.

Mom   : Namsu, it's (1)_____ to (2)_____ your
          (3)_____ .

Namsu : (4)_____ I (5)_____ TV first?

Mom   : No, do (6)_____ homework (7)_____ .
          (8)_____ watch TV (9)_____ .

Namsu : (10)_____ .

PROJECT

Make your own sentences.

Q: What's your idea?

It's time to...

7:00 a.m.

8:00

9:00

11:00

12:00

3:30 p.m.

5:00

7:00

9:00

11:00

LESSON 16

So Long, Everyone!

① take care of ___돌보다___

② kindergarten _____

③ elementary school

_____

④ middle school _____

⑤ high school _____

⑥ university _____

⑦ graduation _____

⑧ celebrate _____

⑨ keep in touch _____

♣ farewell ___이별, 환송___

♣ Congratulations

_____

♣ college _____

♣ So long _____

♣ miss _____

♣ Cheer up _____

♣ look after _____

♣ go back ___돌아가다___

 Look and Listen

Listen and fill in the blanks.

Nami's mom : Congratulations!

Joon : Thank you!

Nami's mom : What _____ school are you going to?

Joon : Daehan Middle School.

Jinho : We're going to the _____ school.

Nami's mom : That's great.

Mrs. Smith : _____, Jinho!

Jinho : Thank you very much.

I'll _____ you, Mrs. Smith.

Mrs. Smith : I'll _____ you, too.

_____ _____ !

Jinho : Thank you.

Mrs. Smith : _____ _____, everyone!

Good-bye!

Children : Good-bye, Mrs. Smith.

 Look and Speak

 Look at the dialogues and speak in English.

A

🎤 진호 김!

👩 축하한다, 진호야!

🧑 정말 감사합니다.

👫 축하한다!

🧑 축하해!

🧑 고마워!

B

🐵 이제 헤어질 시간이구나, 나미야.

🧒 너는 뉴욕으로 다시 돌아가는 거니?

🐵 응, 그래. 잘 있어, 진호야. 잘 있어, 나미야.

🧒🧑 잘 지내, 케빈.
우리는 네가 보고 싶을 거야.

🐵 나도 너희들이 그리울 거야.
모두들 잘 있어! 모두 사랑한다!

🧑 또 보자, 나미야.

🧒 또 다시 보자.

Let's Write

A **Listen to the dialogue again and answer the questions.**

1. Where is everyone now? _____

2. What are they celebrating? _____

3. Which middle school does Jinho go to?

_____

4. Do Jinho and Joon go to different middle school?

_____

B **Answer these questions.**

1. What elementary school are you studying at now?

_____

2. What grade are you in?

_____

3. What is the name of your homeroom teacher?

_____

4. How many students are studying in your class?

_____

5. Are you happy to be in your class?

_____

C **Write in English using "going to..."**

1. 나는 서울 중학교에 갈 거야.   → _____
2. 그는 내일 서울로 돌아갈 거야.   → _____
3. 우리는 새 컴퓨터를 살 거야.   → _____
4. 그들은 런던을 방문할 거야.   → _____
5. 우리는 수학을 공부할 거야.   → _____

Easy Grammar

Make sentences using the given words.

study French (I)	I am going to study French.
read the newspaper (I)	I am going to read the newspaper.
eat salad (She)	She is going to eat salad.

- I <u>am</u> going to...
- You <u>are</u> going to...
- He/She <u>is</u> going to...
- We <u>are</u> going to...
- They <u>are</u> going to...

1. buy a present (I)

_____

2. do my homework (I)

_____

3. do his homework (He)

_____

4. try *Kimchi* (He)

_____

5. play tennis (She)

_____

6. watch a movie (We)

_____

7. wash the car (You)

_____

8. study English (They)

_____

9. read a book (You)

_____

Hansel and Gretel

Gretel	I'm cold.
Hansel	The fire is out. Let's go home. But.. where are the breadcrumbs?
Gretel	I'm cold.
Hansel	Look! There is a house.
Gretel	The house is good to eat.
Witch	Ahh!! Come in!

(The witch put Hansel into a cage.)

Gretel	Oh, my God! You can't put Hansel in a cage!
Witch	Hee, hee, hee.. Yes, I can. I want to eat Hansel first.
Witch	Hee, hee, hee.. Let me light a fire. Is the fire hot?
Gretel	It looks hot. Come and have a look.
Witch	Mmm.. It is hot. Hee, hee, hee..
Gretel	In you go.
Witch	*(screaming)* *(Bang!)*
Gretel	Hansel! The witch is in the fire! We can go home.
Hansel	Thank you. Let's go home.
Gretel	Look! Here is some treasure.
Hansel	Let's get the treasure.

(They got the treasure and found the way home.)

Hansel and Gretel	Daddy, we're home!
Dad	Hansel and Gretel! Ho.. *(crying)* It's good to have you home.. I'm sorry.

Don't Eat the Furniture

Word Bank

twin sons 쌍둥이 아들

in one's arms ~의 품에

stand 서다

closely 가까이

piece 조각

crib 유아용 침대

missing 없어지는, 사라지는

chew 씹다

furniture 가구

worry 걱정하다

swallow 삼키다

wood 나무, 목재

wooden 나무로 된

dirt 먼지, 흙

plant 식물

yard 마당

finally 마침내

find out 알아내다

important 중요한

mineral 미네랄

immediately 곧

prescribe 처방하다

medicine 약

The woman has twin sons. Their names are Ragan and Autumn Beavers. Ragan is in his mother's arms. Autumn is standing in his bed. Look closely at their bed. Little pieces of the crib are missing. They are missing because Autumn ate them.

When Autumn and Ragan were 15 months old, they began to chew on the furniture. At first the twins' mother wasn't worried much. All babies chew on things. But the Beavers twins never stopped. And every time they chewed on the furniture, they swallowed the wood.

First the twins chewed on their beds. Their mother moved the beds out of the twins' bedroom. Then the twins ate the wooden handles on their cabinets. Their mother moved the cabinets out of the bedroom. There wasn't any wooden furniture in the bedroom, so the twins began to eat the door.

The twins also ate dirt. When they were in the house, they ate dirt from the plants and flowers. When they were outside, they ate dirt in the yard. They kept eating wood and dirt.

Finally the twins' mother took them to the doctor. The doctor did some tests. What did the doctor find out? The twins didn't have important minerals. Wood and dirt have these minerals, so the twins ate wood and dirt. The doctor immediately prescribed some medicine. The twins took the medicine, and they stopped eating wood and dirt.

A **Match the underlined pronouns with the correct nouns.**

a. medicine / b. Autumn and Ragan / c. the cabinet/ d. minerals / e. dirt

1. <u>They</u> ate wood and dirt. _____

2. <u>It</u> had wooden handles. _____

3. The twins ate <u>it</u> in the yard. _____

4. <u>Wood</u> and dirt have them. _____

5. The twins need to take <u>it</u>. _____

B **Find the wrong words and cross them out. Then write the correct words.**

Look closely at the ~~desk~~. Little pieces of the crib are missing. → <u>bed</u>

1. At first the twins' mother wasn't worried much. All babies scratch on things.
   → _____

2. When they were in the house, they ate dirt from the ground. → _____

3. The twins didn't have important books.   → _____

4. The twins don't need to eat wood and dirt anymore. They need to take their sandwich and salad.   → _____

LET'S HAVE FUN

Word Puzzle

→ Across

2. I'm going back (   ) New York tomorrow.
4. I like (   ) computer games.
7. Would you (   ) to come to my house?
8. That's (   ) I am going.
11. What middle (   ) are you going to?
12. I'll (   ) you, too.
14. I am 13 years (   ).
16. So long! Everyone! I love (   ) all.

↓ Down

1. So (   ), everyone!
3. What (   ) school are you going to?
5. I go to the park (   ) 3:30.
6. What (   ) do you go to school?
9. Please say (   ) to your family.
10. What time do you (   ) to bed?
11. We're going to the (   ) school.
13. Please (   ) hello to your family.
15. Thank you very (   ).

Board Game

🍃 **ACTIVITY**

reviewing the words from lesson 1 to lesson 16

🍃 **WORD**

all the words that you know

🍃 **EXPRESSION**

• make them any sentences freely

A Fill in the blanks with the right words.

1. I'm going to _____ back to Korea next month.

2. They are going to _____ grandparents for *Chu-seok*.

3. We are going to _____ a new car this week.

4. He's going to _____ a test tomorrow.

5. I'm going to _____ an interesting history book tonight.

6. Are you going to _____ cold water?

7. Is he going to _____ a bus to school?

8. Is she going to _____ a letter to her friend in Japan?

9. Are you going to _____ the window?

10. Are they going to _____ storybooks?

B Find the opposite word and match them.

1. same   •   • a. short

2. going   •   • b. sad

3. say hello   •   • c. coming

4. long   •   • d. say good-bye

5. happy   •   • e. different

6. last   •   • f. hate

7. like   •   • g. first

Choose the correct answer.

1. _____ on your graduation.

   a. Thanks   b. Welcome   c. Miss   d. Congratulations

2. So _____ , everyone.

   a. short   b. long   c. come   d. go

3. What middle school are you _____ to?

   a. going   b. go   c. went   d. to go

4. _____ care, Kevin.

   a. Have   b. Take   c. Get   d. Set

5. I live _____ Seoul, Korea.

   a. on   b. off   c. from   d. in

Listen and fill in the blanks.

Kevin	: (1)_____ to say (2)_____, Nami.
Nami	: Are you going (3)_____ to New York?
Kevin	: Yes, I (4)_____. Good-bye, Jinho.
	Good-bye, Nami.
Jinho, Nami	: (5)_____ _____, Kevin.
	We'll (6)_____ you.
Kevin	: I'll miss you, too.
	(7)_____ _____, everyone!
	I (8)_____ you all!
Jinho	: (9)_____ you, Nami.
Nami	: See you (10)_____.
Children	: Good-bye, Mrs. Smith.

PROJECT

Q: **What** are you going to do first when you become age 20?

Friend's name	I'm going to...